ISBN 978-0-260-87855-7
PIBN 10979802

Forgotten Books is a registered trademark of FB &c Ltd.
Copyright © 2018 FB &c Ltd.
FB &c Ltd, Dalton House, 60 Windsor Avenue, London, SW19 2RR.
Company number 08720141. Registered in England and Wales.

For support please visit www.forgottenbooks.com

ye Hornᴇ Book of ye Art Faire

In Secret Studie, then Such work he 'gan devise
As might his conning best commend and please
the looker's eye.
Tottle's Miscellany.

# ROYAL CANADIAN ACADEMY OF ARTS

## FOUNDERS:
The Marquis of Lorne & The Princess Louise

## PATRON:
His Excellency The Marquis of Lansdowne
Governor General of Canada

## OFFICERS
President . L.R.O'Brien Toronto . Vice-President A.C. Hutchison, Montreal
Secretary (Jas. Smith. Toronto . Auditor Henry Langley. Toronto
& Treasurer)

## Council . 1888-89
Frank Darling, Toronto . M. Matthews, Toronto .
O.R. Jacobi, Montreal . J.W. Hopkins, Montreal
H. Langley, Toronto . J.C. Forbes, Toronto
Wm Bayne, Montreal . Jos. Connolly, Toronto
Forshaw Day. Kingston . D. Fowler, Amherst Island
H. Perré, Toronto . J.W.H Watts. Ottawa

## Honorary Retired Academicians

Mons Playmondon      Quebec.
J. C. Howard      Toronto.

## Academicians

| | | | |
|---|---|---|---|
| N. Bourassa | Montreal. | A. C. Hutchison | Montreal. |
| W. Brymner | Montreal. | O. R. Jacobi | Montreal |
| Gos Connolly | Toronto | Henry Langley | Toronto |
| W. N. Cresswell | Seaforth | M. Matthews | Toronto |
| Forshaw Day | Kingston | T. M. Martin | Toronto |
| F. Darling | Toronto | L. R. O'Brien | Toronto |
| Allan Eason | Montreal | A. Perré | Toronto |
| D. Fowler | Amherst Island | William Raphael. | Montreal |
| T. Fuller. | Ottawa | T. A. Scott | Ottawa |
| J. A. Fraser | Ottawa | F. M. Bell-Smith | London Ont |
| J. S. Forbes | Toronto | James Smith | Toronto |
| James Griffiths | London | W. G. Storm | Toronto |
| R. Harris | Montreal | J. W. H. Watts | Ottawa |
| L. P. Hebert | Montreal | A. R. Watson | Door |
| J. W. Hopkins | Montreal | D. F. Woodcock | Montreal |
| A. H. Howard | Toronto | Patterson A. D. | Toronto |

## Honorary Non-Resident Academicians

S. S. Millard      Cheltenham Eng
G. J. Way      Lausanne Switzerland
H. Y. Sandham      Boston U.S.

## ASSOCIATES

| | | | |
|---|---|---|---|
| Bird, A. | Montreal | Miles, J.C. | St. Johns, N.B. |
| Boisseau, A | Ottawa | Peel, P.A.D | London, Ont |
| Cox, A, | Toronto | Pinhey, J.C. | Ottawa |
| FORSTER, J.W.L | Toronto | Reid, G.A. | Toronto |
| GAGEN, R.F. | Toronto | Revel, Wm. | Toronto |
| Gordon, F.C. | Brockville | Rolph, J.T | Toronto |
| Hannaford, M. | Toronto | Ruel, W.H | Wooton. Eng |
| Harvey, Geo. | Halifax | Shrapnel, E.S | Whitby. |
| Jones, Miss. F.M. | Halifax | Shuttleworth, E.B. | Toronto |
| Lawson, J.K. | Toroto | Whale, Robert. | Brantford, Ont |
| McCarthy, H. | Toronto | Windeat. Emma. S. | Toronto |
| Martin, Henry. | Hamilton | | |

## Associate Designer

| | |
|---|---|
| Ellis, Jno. | Toronto |
| McCausland. Robt. | Toronto |
| Willing, J.T. | Toronto |

## Associate Architects

| | | | |
|---|---|---|---|
| Balfour, James. | Hamilton | Gemmel, John | Toronto |
| Busch, H.E. | Halifax | Gordon, H. | Toronto |
| Burke, E | Toronto | Harris, W.C | Winnipeg |
| Chesterton, W. | Ottawa | McNicol, R. | Winnipeg |
| Curry, S.G. | Toronto | McKean, J.T.C. | St. Johns, N.B |
| Dick, D.B. | Toronto | Nelson, Jas | Montreal |
| Dewar, Andrew. | Halifax | Steele, A.D | Montreal |
| Dunlop, A.F. | Montreal | Taylor, A.T | Montreal |
| Durand, George. | London, Ont | Windeyer, R.C | Toronto |
| Gage, R. | Kingston | | |

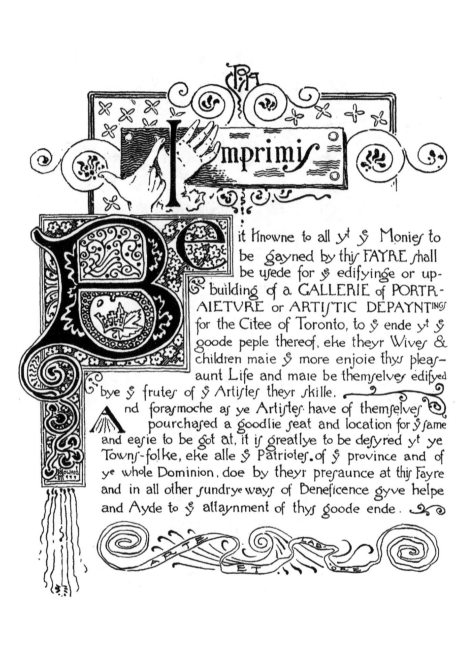

# Imprimis

**B**e it knowne to all y$^t$ $\check{y}$ Monies to be gayned by this FAYRE shall be usede for $\check{y}$ edifyinge or up-building of a GALLERIE of PORTR-AIETVRE or ARTISTIC DEPAYNT$^{ings}$ for the Citee of Toronto, to $\check{y}$ ende y$^t$ $\check{y}$ goode peple thereof, eke theyr Wives & children maie $\check{y}$ more enjoie thys pleasaunt Life and maie be themselves edifyed bye $\check{y}$ frutes of $\check{y}$ Artistes theyr skille.

**A**nd forasmoche as ye Artistes have of themselves pourchased a goodlie seat and location for $\check{y}$ same and easie to be got at, it is greatlye to be desyred y$^t$ ye Towns-folke, eke alle $\check{y}$ Patriotes of $\check{y}$ province and of ye whole Dominion, doe by theyr presaunce at this Fayre and in all other sundrye ways of Beneficence gyve helpe and Ayde to $\check{y}$ attaynment of thys goode ende.

THE POEM

Did ever on painter's canvas live
The power of his fancy's dream?
Did ever poet's pen achieve
Fruition of his theme?
Did ever marble take the life
That the sculptor's soul conceived?
Or ambition win in passion's strife
What its glowing hopes believed?
Did ever racer's eager feet
Rest as he reached the goal,
Finding the prize achieved was meet
To satisfy the soul?

Daniel Wilson

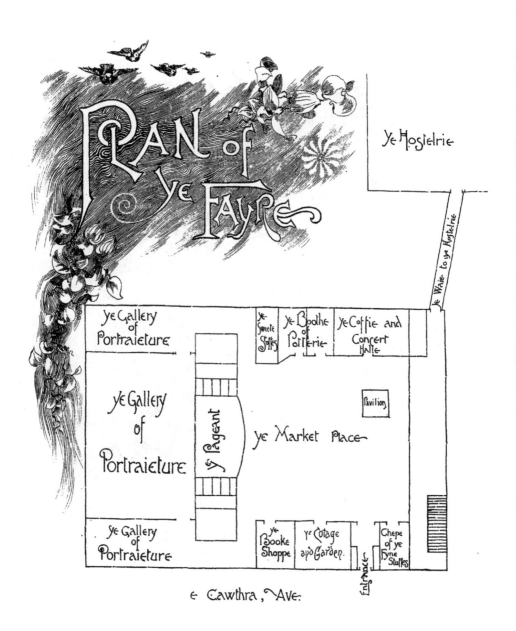

Plan of ye Fayre

Ye Hostelrie

Walk to ye Hostelrie

ye Gallery of Portraicture

Ye Sweete Stalles

Ye Boothe of Potterie

Ye Coffie and Concert Halle

ye Gallery of Portraicture

ye Pageant

Pavilion

ye Market Place

ye Gallery of Portraicture

ye Booke Shoppe

ye Cotage and Garden

Entrance

Chepe of ye Fyne Stuffes

← Cawthra Ave.

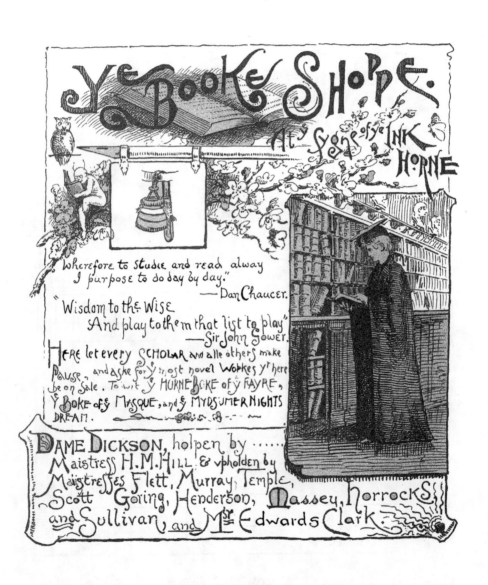

# YE BOOKE SHOPPE.

## At ye Signe of ye INK HORNE

"Wherefore to studie and read alway
I purpose to do day by day."
— Dan Chaucer.

"Wisdom to the WISE
And play to them that list to play"
— Sir John Gower.

HERE let every SCHOLAR and alle others make
Pause, and aske for ye most novel Workes yt here
be on Sale. To wit ye HURNEBOKE of ye FAYRE,
ye BOKE of ye MASQUE, and ye MYDSUMER NIGHTS
DREAM.

DAME DICKSON, holpen by ......
Maistress H. M. HILL & upholden by
Maistresses Flett, Murray, Temple,
Scott Goring, Henderson, Massey, Horrocks,
and Sullivan, and Mrs Edwards Clark.

CONCERT AND COFFEE HALLE.
ATTE SYGNE OF YE
CAT AND FIDDLE

Refreshments for
Men and Beast
Musick by ye Merrie Minstrels
after Curfew.

DAMES BAINES
FORSYTH, GRANT, holpen
and vpholden by .......
Dames DOUGLAS ARMOVR
Torrence and McKelcan,
with Maistresses
Todd, M. Todd,
Hendrie, Spratt,
Armstrong, Langmuir,
Benson and
Dolly Armour.

# Ye Cotage and Garden

At ye Signe of ye Travellers Joy
"Sweete variety must still delight."
Lope de Vego.

"A woman always did from the first make a muss in a garden." C.D. Warner.

Ladies Nordheimer, Cassels, and Vernon, holpen by ye Mistresses Marjorie Campbell, Selina Vernon, Maud Yarker and May Dawson.

As soon as you come in to the Fayre turne to the right and so perceive ye Cotage withe ye Garden of lovelie and swete scented flowers. And herein shall ye not see cloathes of Arras to cover ye walles, nor store of plate to discover anie wealth, for ye simple villagers use neither to be proud nor covetous: you shall find heere cheese and Milk for dainties, and wooll for cleathing eke ye Spining Wheele, wereby ye busie housewife doth prepare the same, And ever and anon ye-ye Fayre Maydens do looke forth of ye lattice to gage upon ye diversions of ye Fayre.

Ye PAVILION

KEPTE By

DAMES
Drayton and Cattanach
Holpen By

Misstresses O'Brien, Meredith, Ardagh, Kathleen O'Brien,
Florence Cole, Sallie Mickle, an Violet Smith.

Ye Boothe of Fyne STUFFES
At Sygne of ye TABARD

Costly thy habit as
thy purse can buye
SHAKESPEARE

Dame d'Auria
Holpen By Misstresses
Catto and McGee

Ye Boothe of Sweet Meats
at ye signe of ye Sugar Loafe

"Sweetes with
Sweetes war
not;
Joy·
delights in
Joy."

— Shakespeare.

Danne Skae holpen by
Mistress Rutherford, and
upholden by Mistress Gilder-steve
Stevenson, Oslet
and Skae

Ye Hostelrie at ye Signe of ye Star and Garter

"Shall I not take mine ease in mine Inn?"
Sir J. Falstaff.

Ye Strangers in need of REFRESHMENT after alle ye QUAINTE SIGHTS of y FAYRE shall fynde very excellente goode entertaynment in y HOSTELRIE AT Y Signe depicted above.

Kepte By

Dame Strachan. Dame Hosking. Dame McMurray. Dame Williamson. Dame Lee. Dame Muttlebury. Dame Evans. Dame Parsons. Dame Fanar. Dame Hodgins. with other fair Damosels and Sprightly Damozels

# Ye Boothe of Glasse and China-Ware

At ye Signe of ye Glass-Blower

Buy, buy, buy, come buy, come buy. Here be ye pretious wares of ye glass-blower, his art, brought from beyonde seas. Ye Fayre-ones eke maie here catche sighte of their lovely faces, which do so much whette both ye artiste his skille and Cupid his arrows.

## DAME MacMAHON.

Holpen and upholden by

Misstresses

Birchall. Howden, and Bolster.

"GLASSES. GLASSES, IS the ONLY Drinking" Falstaff.

ye **YSTE OF DIVERS ENTERTAINEMENTS OF SWEETE MUSICK**

Item ye **GYPTIANS**
Ye Egipciens or Gypsies from Bohemia, out of
attired after ye manner of theyr nation
shall sing under conduct of Dame Hillary to a rare & full
musick

Item ye **QUEENES GLEEMEN**
Ye Singers of her Majesty will eke appear
with theyr overseer Master Schuch, where-
by ye place shall be filled with ye very food of love, musick to witte

Item ye **SINGEING MEN**
A concert of singyng men under theyr leader
Master F. H. Torrington will furnish forth
harmonies full of excellente delyte & change

Item ye **SCHOLER-MUSICIANS**
Ye Schole or Conservatorie of Musick shall
under leave of Master Edward Fisher, pro-
vide curiouslie devysed entertainement wherein ye
singers shall be attired after ye antique maner

Item ye **MINSTRASIE**
Master Will. E. Haslam with his Minstrels,
Masters alle of ye gaie science will further
charm ye lovers of sweete sounds by music most quaint
& curious

"Here will we sit & let the sound of Music
Creep in our ears".
Merchant of Venice

The best in this kind are but shadows;
And the worst are no worse if imagination amend them.

# FAYRIE PAGEANT

## ADAPTED FROM WILL SHAKSPEARE HIS
## MIDSUMER NIGHT DREAME

### BY DAME C. MORRISON
### WITH MENDELSSOHN HIS MUSIAK
### ARRANGED AND TAUGHT BY
### MASTER JAMES PLUMMER

## YE CAST OF CHARACTERS

FAIRIES

| | | |
|---|---|---|
| OBERON. King of Fairies | Mistress | C. JARVIS |
| TITARIA. Queen | " | E. JARVIS |
| 1st FAIRY | " | PATTERSON |
| 2nd " | " | LARMONT |
| PUCK or Robin Goodfellow. | Master | W. P. MOSS |

MORTAL

NICK BOTTOM the Weaver · C. MOSS

Attendant Elves & Fairies upon the King

## MUSIA

Solo & Chorus "Over Hill over Dale"

Duet "I know a bank"

Solo "My true love hath my heart"
(a ditty of Sir Phillip Sydney)

Concerted finale and Epilogue

Through the house give glimmering light

# Ye Masque of May Days

"for Summer and his pleasures wait on thee"
Shakspere

"Acting in song, especially in dialogues hath an extreme good grace"
Bacon

WHEREIN three several Companies & to wit, FORTUNES DARLINGS of ye COURTE, Ye COUNTRIE MUMMERS, and ROBIN and his MERRIEMEN shall all make disporte together with songs and dancing AROUND ye MAIE POLE. AND here shall be somewhat beholden to ye shrewde observer how CUPIDE is wont to plague his VICTIMS AND yt he may the more profit thereby he is counm-sailed to BUY for HIMSELF and his LADIE

Ye Booke of ye MASQUE to be found at ye SYGNE OF YE INKHORN

ỹ Maye Queene

Robin Hood
and ye Jolly Friar

ỹ Masque
of Maye Daie
Contrived By
Dame Harrison
Holpen By
Dame Fitzgibbon.

G. A. Reid.

ye Measure or ye Minuet in honour of Englands Glorious Victorie

I must believe some miracles still be
When Sydney's name I hear or face I see
— Ben Johnson

Tis ye eve of St John - in ye great
halle of Penshurst - ye lights burn low
Ye great castle Bell tolls midnight
& lo! at that magic sound
the pictures live
Music is floating
in the air
Ye halle is filled
with Light
& for one shorte hour ye courtlye dames
and nobles mingle in ye statelie dance
But darkness grows again & in the
fadinglight they sadlye turne them
each one to his place to wait a yeare
the tolling of that bell that calls them
back to life

CPSIA information can be obtained
at www.ICGtesting.com
Printed in the USA
BVHW031224021118
531991BV00008B/813/P

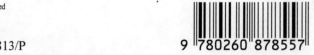